CREATE REALITY, INC.
Presents:
A MANAGER'S MIND

THE FOUNDATION FOR ENTRY-LEVEL MANAGEMENT

By
Christian J. Evans

Published by
CREATE REALITY, INC.
PO BOX 9665
PEORIA, IL 61612-9665
Phone: 309-648-5355
www.createreality-inc.com
createreality_llc@yahoo.com

authorHOUSE™

1663 LIBERTY DRIVE, SUITE 200
BLOOMINGTON, INDIANA 47403
(800) 839-8640
WWW.AUTHORHOUSE.COM

AuthorHouse™
1663 Liberty Drive, Suite 200
Bloomington, IN 47403
www.authorhouse.com
Phone: 1-800-839-8640

AuthorHouse™ UK Ltd.
500 Avebury Boulevard
Central Milton Keynes, MK9 2BE
www.authorhouse.co.uk
Phone: 08001974150

First published by AuthorHouse 2/17/2006

ISBN: 1-4259-0206-5 (sc)

Printed in the United States of America
Bloomington, Indiana

This book is printed on acid-free paper.

A MANAGER'S MIND –THE FOUNDATION FOR ENTRY- LEVEL MANAGEMENT
Copyright © 2005 by Christian J. Evans
Library of Congress copyright code- Txu1-245-668

All photographs by www.f8studio.net

Contents

Chapter Four

Chapter Five

Closure

Notes and Quotes

Additional Information

Thank Yous

First and foremost, I would like to thank **GOD** for being the head of my life and blessing me everyday I open my eyes. I am thankful for everything that He has done for my family and me. I want to thank Him for giving me my gift.

I want to thank my mother for everything, and I mean everything. I cannot put in words what she means to me. Love you *Mom!* Love you *Grandma!*

To Pastor and Prophet Jackie & Victoria Adams: I love you both. I thank both of you for supporting me through all my years. Through your teachings, you have taught me to put GOD first to take control of what is in front of me. You have been a true example of how to live in GODLINESS and LOVE, and to be UPRIGHT and in UNITY as long as I've known you.

To my brother Julius: For being there in every situation, and for always pushing me to go to the next level, to be one step ahead of the rest. Thank you for encouraging me, and believing in my visions. You have the best music in the world. I say that without a second's hesitation. The Enzo is yours!

To my brothers, *Clifton, William, and Jon:* I learn from you all. Sometimes a headache but every day there's love there.

To my cousins, *TJ and Shun:* For being such comics. You both need your own stand-up show.

To Uncle Eric & Monica: For all the intangible things you've done.

To Mrs. Deborah Flowers: For always speaking the word "entrepreneur" over my life. See you in heaven.

I would like to thank myself for completing this project. The best is yet to come.

Thank YOU for supporting this project.

Introduction

DEFINITIONS

The Hand- Tan represents a multi-cultural hand. Mixture of all races on the earth becoming one race: the human race.

Lettering and Water- Green represents land and growth. The land unites us all.

™**Continents**- Blue continents represent less separation by the continents being water. It is a twist on the norm. The world you create is in your hands.

WHAT DOES IT MEAN?
CREATE: *"to bring into existence"*
REALITY: *"the quality or state of being real"*

WHAT IS IT?

CREATE REALITY is a company and a movement. We all hold our world in our hands. Whatever we see in front of us, it's because we created it in one form or another. Our actions and reactions to situations determine our future. These buildings, cars, or houses did not magically appear overnight. Someone created them in their imagination and produced them into reality. The world is founded on these principles. In Genesis 1:27, it states,

> "So God **created** man in his own image
> **[imagination]**, in the image of God he
> created him; male and female he created
> them."

So, in turn, aren't we supposed to do the same thing: use our imagination to create?

THE COMPANY

Whatever is in our imagination, we will bring it to existence for the world, whether it's books, clothes, movies, or inventions. This is to encourage you that through **_GOD_** you can do anything!

THE MOVEMENT

Our imagination is a medium from one world to another. People imagine what they want to do, places they want to go, and how successful they want to be, but only a select few push themselves enough to see it become reality. Whenever you see the CREATE REALITY logo, it is to encourage you to do the same thing. Push yourself to see your dreams come true. Do not sit back and let life pass you by. Do something about it.

CREATE REALITY
IT'S A VERB!

Christian J. Evans
President & CEO
CREATE REALITY, INC.
P.O. BOX 9665
PEORIA, IL 61612-9665
309-648-5355
www.createreality-inc.com
createreality_inc@yahoo.com

Hello, my name is Christian Evans and you have picked this book to help you begin your new role as a manager. This is a beginner's guide to what you will go through and experience. In no way is this based on stats or someone who hasn't been through it himself. This is a book based on successful experience. The most important part of any building or home is its foundation, and this reading is your foundation. There are plenty of books about the dos and don'ts of a manager but this is phase one of many. I lived by the saying *"EVERY DAY IT'S SOMETHING."* Everyday will present a different challenge for you. No two days are the same. You have to embed that statement in your brain, just to prepare you for the ever-changing days to come. It could be anything from employee issues, vendors, product, or maintenance.

I had been the general manager of a nationally respected pizza chain for two years, but have worked for this company overall for five years. Going from the bottom to the top was a challenge in itself. I know how it is to be an employee, what they go through, and what I was looking for in my manager. I've been on both sides of the coin. When the opportunity came to be the GM, I was hesitant at first, but soon agreed to the position. I knew a chance like this only comes so often, so I seized the moment. Upon taking my role as GM, I was excited about my job. I loved the essence of business and its functions

In my time, I was successful, receiving financial promotions and advancing rapidly through store operations such as cleanliness, labor, low employee turnover, and sales increase. I was told that I had a lot on my plate to deal with in my future position but I did not take heed to it too much. I wanted to take it day by day. At the time, I was a fresh twenty-one-year-old coming into a fairly good amount of money as well as responsibilities. I think if I had known about a book such as this, it would have helped me to prepare for what was to come.

After my time as GM, I became an assistant manager at another national pizza chain. (I must like pizza, huh?) This one offered full service, with a dining room and table service, and all that. I'm not one to job hop, but it was my situation at the time. Both had the same concept for the manager to operate. I have decided to share my experiences with you because I know you may be looking for help as I once was. Hopefully, I can be of some assistance to you. Within this book, I will attempt to share everything I can with you: the good, the bad, and the ugly. You will learn time management skills, the importance of customer service, employee discipline/rewards, how to hold yourself as a professional, and to create overall confidence in your leadership.

The most challenging aspect of management is people management. People management covers employees, vendors, and customers. You will be dealing with these people more than you will with the business. You need all three to work effectively to run a successful operation. Without them, you will have nothing, so take good care of them. Oh yeah: if you don't have a mobile phone by now, please get one. You will be on call 24/7 for multiple reasons. (Just thought I'd let you in on that one.)

There are also many perks to being a manager, too many to put in words. For the most part, you dictate your hours, maybe receive free or discounted products, or you enjoy the look on people's faces when they know you're in charge. This position you hold comes with a great deal of power. Do not take this to your head. This is a quick way to ruin the ability for things to work for, with, and around you. Ego-tripping is the number one no-no at this level. Take the power you have and have fun with it. Utilize it to do great things. Have confidence! Do not be afraid to take a chance or to make a mistake (this is a great experience tool). Be honest to your people, and make the most out of what you do. The knowledge you will gain from your experiences is something no school curriculum on any level can teach you. You will determine how far you will go. My duty is to show you the door and key.

Chapter One

Customer Service

They say you're supposed to save the best for last, but if I were to put this at the end, everything that you would have read would have been meaningless. If you do not have this first, you will have no business. I feel this is the most important chapter of this book, so it shall go first.

Customer service is everything you see, hear, feel, and smell. From the time a shopper arrives at your establishment, everything should be ideal for him or her. Is the parking lot clean? Are the outside garbage cans emptied? Has any litter been picked up? Are the windows clean? These are the things being analyzed. You have to remember that you are also a customer. To truly have the eyes of the manager, you also need the eyes of the customer. Be able to identify what they are aware of during their visit. They're aware of anything and everything, from an employee's attitude, grooming, and personal hygiene, to whether or not you have customer-friendly music being played, to the basic cleanliness of the store. Treat every customer as if they were royalty. Never tell them, *"No," "We don't have it,"* or *"I don't know."* If you don't know, then immediately follow up with, ***"Let me check that for you."*** If you don't have it, then assure them ***you will try everything within your power to get it for them.***

In Chapter 2, I will explain how to look at customers as walking money. These people are paying you to serve them. Consider it an honor that out of the gazillion places in the world they could have gone to spend their dollar, they chose to come to you. You have what they want (product); they have what you need (money and word of mouth). It is simple as that. Every time they come, you give, and provide generously, everything in your power to guarantee their return. **Honorable service times, friendly staff/environment, and quality of product are the formula for customer return and over-the-top service.**

SERVICE TIMES

Honor the service times you give your clientele. If there will be a wait on what they need, then be honest and tell them, and take the time to explain <u>why</u> it will take that amount of time. You will get the customer that much more involved in the process it takes to produce their product. Customers feel better knowing the *slight* extra amount of time was spent wisely to see that it was done appropriately. The worst thing to do is to have them wait and still deliver an incorrect product. They feel they have wasted their time with you, and will feel disrespected that you wasted their valuable time. Shame on you! If it takes you telling them it may take an extra day or couple of minutes for sugar (but you know you will get it to them earlier than that) then that is OK. Getting it to them earlier than what you said is even better.

FRIENDLY STAFF AND ENVIRONMENT

Create an atmosphere where customers feel relaxed and comfortable. It starts with your staff, and you hire your staff. You will be in charge of the people you employ. You will be responsible if you let a bad apple in the bunch. (Some won't show their true colors till later on down the road. With a good eye, you can pick them out.) When you interview, screen these people to see if they even have a pulse. You want to have a team of people who are energetic and have superb personalities. Chemistry is important among you and your staff. I'm telling you right now, from personal experience, that the person you are consider hiring from a past interview, the one who was quiet, who had the look on their face that said, "Don't talk to me at all," but who has good work experience, will cause you more problems in the long run. You have to look at it like this: with the proper training and attention, you should be able to teach a monkey how to do what your staff has to do. That person may work well for you, but not well for the customers. Remember: Customers are your bosses and you will have more complaints or comments about that person. You will bend head-over-heels fighting for that person trying to explain why they are the way they are and no one wants to hear it. Save yourself some future time, and get the right one for the customer.

Once you get the correct mix of people who will help you deliver over-the-top service, you will be ready for the world. We will go in depth with hiring and staffing in Chapter 3. You are the boss. STAMP IT IN YOUR BRAIN!!!!! After my promotion to GM, you wouldn't believe how long it took me to realize that. Your staff is looking up to you for your leadership and direction. That is what a boss is: a leader. You set the standards, from smiles, to uniforms, to greetings. Anything you do, whether positive or negative, will have a trickle-down effect. Before every shift, have a pre-game huddle explaining strategy. Check attitudes at the door. This will be the time if they need to let off steam or voice opinions and concerns. You do not want them dealing with the public holding any resentment of something that happened in the establishment or personal, affecting your service. A lot of times, when employees have a problem, they just need someone to talk to and vent. All you have to do is *listen*. Make the employees feel at ease to come to work. They have to know that work needs to be done, but realize that this is their second home and they are in this together with you. Try to do as much for them as they do for you, but remember they are working and servicing you also. They have to see you have concern and care for them, and in return they will give it back to the customer. It's in the almighty WORD, "You get what you put in."

QUALITY PRODUCT

You sell, they buy; what they buy has to be to their standards. If they want a hammer, then give them the best hammer they have ever had. If it is a hot plate of noodles, make certain that the best ingredients were used to prepare it. A lot of businesses think that making a defective product to keep their money coming in (you wouldn't believe how some prey on the weak and desperate) and flowing is a way for them to keep their money coming back. This is not true. How many times have you had a product go wrong on you, or it was not what you hoped for? By this time, you are mad enough to call and complain, or if you are too busy, never to buy it again and tell everyone you know not to buy it. For every bad experience a customer has, they tell at least ten people. Those ten people tell ten more, and so on, and so on. Eventually, you will find someone who can offer you the same service, but a better overall product. You may stick with that company and become a regular customer, as long as they keep giving you that Grade-A product, and then you will tell ten more of your friends. Now, look yourself in the mirror and ask yourself which company do you want to run? Can you guess with whom it starts? BINGO: YOU. Your standards need to be so concrete that during the preparation of the product, everyone is following the exact specifications on how the product is made. There can be no shortcuts on what it takes to make what you make. There are no shortcuts in quality. A shortcut in productions can mean a shortcut in your sales. Remember what I said about taking your time with product if needed? Do not, and I repeat *do not*, stray from it. The advice I give you will save you countless man hours following up with the employee who rushed the product, or on customer complaint calls, and you pulling your hair out once you see that your sales have gone down.

You will soon find out there are many working parts in your operation needed to complete one goal. Everything is a cycle, in one form or another, and everything will come back to you sooner or later. You have the easy part of the deal. You have to oversee that each station, person, and/or department is doing the job correctly for the final result. As much as you would think on how easy this process is, then you may as well close this book right now. It will take a firm person — like you — to ensure that it is done the right way. When you are dealing with people, some more than others have their own way on how they feel the product should be and how to get it done. Your staff has the customers' product in their hands, and this is when you — the captain — will step in, put your foot down, and say, "This is how it is done." On the same hand, be open for suggestions and be ready to evaluate if a tweak in the system could help you make it better and faster. All three steps will help you accomplish over-the-top service if executed correctly. I can't put it in any particular order in terms of which is most important, but I do know it starts with you.

Chapter Two

MANAGER'S TIME

YOUR TIME

Your time is the essential key for day-to-day success. You are the leader and people will need you more than ever. In order for you to be available for them, you have to get yourself organized. The demand for an individual — such as yourself — calls for sacrifice. In the beginning of your role, you will put in many hours, many hours of your life that you cannot get back. Look at it this way: you were going to spend that same amount of hours doing something else. It may be more productive, it may not be, but this is the task you took on and this is what comes with it. The personal time you've once had will not disappear; it will be reduced. It is up to you to gain your quality of life back, and it is all in your hands. You will be the one to make your own schedule. You will be in charge of everyone around you. If your people are good, then that will make your job that much easier. The more time you dedicate to your position, the more time you will gain back for yourself. Again, you are in control. You control your own time.

EMPLOYEE'S TIME

The hours your employee's are scheduled and work are vital. Scheduling can be like a Rubik's Cube some weeks. You have to strategically place people when you need them to be the most productive for you and the operation, and at the same time, please them with pay. Some want to work more hours than the others. To that group of people, I say, **"Performance + Attitude = Hours."** It speaks for itself. One of the most damaging aspects in employee time is for you to have them there doing nothing. Always have something for them to do. Have a game plan before they come in, so they're productive from the time they clock in to the time they clock out.

CUSTOMERS' TIME

This is the name of the game. Cutting right to the chase, you need to quote customers slightly longer waiting times so you can have it for them earlier than you told them. This will only make your operation look better. For instance, if you know for a fact that it will take you ten minutes until their order is ready, tell them it will be fifteen. When it is actually to them in ten minutes (or less), they will congratulate you on how fast you are. Speed and quality are what they want in this day and age. Neither should be sacrificed for the other. Have complete balance of the two all the way around. Customers are your bosses; do not waste your boss's time. Your boss could become angry and fire you (not literally, but bad customer service over time could result in no customers at all, and then you won't have a job).

MANAGE PEOPLE

EMPLOYEES

As you will come to find in your work, there will be two kinds of employees: ones who want to work and ones who don't. Their attitude will prove, in their performance, which one they are. Your employees need attention, direction, supervision, and motivation. Let your employees know you are there to help them. In return, you will be the one who will receive the most out of the deal. You gain their trust as well as completing any needed projects. You can't run a business from an office or by pointing fingers. You have to get out there and get it done along with your people. Together Employees And Management = **SUCCESS.** It spells it out right there: **TEAM = SUCCESS.** There is no "I" in TEAM, neither the definition I spelled out. If you are doing great in sales, op cost, or anything else that goes along with the business, it's you and your workers. When you get rewarded, they need to be rewarded also. Create an incentive program for them. Post an "Employee of the Month" picture with the winner's name where everyone can see it — including customers. It's a great motivational tool. Consider spending some of the store's money to purchase product or credit on an item. The idea is up to you. My mother once said, *"You can get more to taste honey than you can vinegar."* It's about how you say it and when. You can't constantly yell or they'll never feel appreciated to work. You need them as well as they need you. It's a win-win situation. Take care of your people and they will take care of you.

CUSTOMERS

When it comes to customers, whenever *"you"* or *"your"* comes up, it is referring to you and your employees. The almighty code is **"the customer is always right."** It is not 100 percent true, but your job is to ensure that they *believe* that they are. Maintaining consistency whenever they visit or purchase anything from you is in your hands. You may not be working on it physically with your hands, but, when you're the manager, you oversee everything. You will always have new customers. This is why you want to ensure consistency in service to make the new customers have the same experience, day in and day out. You will have the ones who want something for free, the ones who call you to complain, or the ones who call and say thank you. It is all how you handle each one. You should look at each customer as walking money. If you like money and what it does, then why would you treat it badly? Oh yeah, money does have feelings: you can treat money badly, by mismanaging it. Isn't it true that if you mismanage money, you will be in the red, bankrupt, or in debt? The contrast to money and customers is like the people on the "get out of debt" commercials. If you treat your customers badly, you will be in debt to them, and debt to them could mean no business for you.

On the other side of the coin, have fun with your customers. Get to know your regulars on a first-name basis. You are the face of the business, and they will be seeing you often if you treat them properly. The amazed look on their faces when they would walk in and I would know their order by heart was enough to make their day. Feel free to ask, *"How's your day going?"* Don't be afraid to carry on a conversation. This will give you a one-on-one relationship with the customer. Think about it: How many businesses are going to ask that question and actually listen? You have to be the one who will listen. Depending on what business you are in, it may be slightly tougher than others. The least you can do is try to make an effort at it. Take it like a losing team in any sport, professional or amateur. There are quite a few teams with losing records, but they still have fans and people cheering them on constantly, and with belief because they're making an effort to become better. Let them see that you are making an effort to make their visit better each time they come. Even if you did nothing wrong, you need to have a mindset of, *"How can I make their next visit that much better?"* **No one is perfect, but that is no excuse not to strive for perfection.**

VENDORS

You are now the vendors' customer. So any praise or complaints you have, that is who you go to. You have to put your "customer" hat on because you are the one purchasing their products and the one who judges quality of it when it arrives and if it arrives on time. Is the delivery driver placing the product in its proper place? Have an open line of communication with your vendor. You will come to find out that they are concerned about the quality of their product to you and how you received it. Knowing the vendor has my quality of mind in mind lets me know they have the same concerns I have. It lets me know that they are ready to listen attentively if I need to talk to them. This is the business world, and if anything out of your hands affects your venture — either in a positive or a negative way — it needs to be addressed. If possible, get the phone numbers of the general manager, district manager, or even the owner, if needed. If you have any concerns with them, it will be helpful to know to whom you need to talk. Otherwise, you will spend countless hours getting your call tossed like a hot potato by people who do not have the proper authority to handle your call. These relationships are what you make of them. Be firm, and remember: You are the customer now, and they will listen.

MANAGE OPERATION

QUALITY

If something looks, smells, or feels bad, then pitch it. Learn to trust your gut when it comes to quality or you will pay for it in the end. Pitching a bad product, rather than selling it to a customer, will save you money in the end. They will not be satisfied with it and can obviously tell what's wrong. They may want a replacement, which means now you're paying for it, through a promotion account. On top of that, the customer may not still be satisfied, so you have to gain their trust all over again. That is a long and pricey process to go through when you could have just pitched it to begin with. Salvaging bad product means nothing when it comes to quality control. Most members of management have bonus programs implemented for them. Usually it is a labor, inventory (product cost), or sales increase. Now, if you have bad product, you have bad customer service. If you have bad customer service, then your sales will decrease. The biggest thing any owner of a business will look at on paper is their sales increase. If they see a slump in their sales, they are going to come to the business you're running to check up on you, in and out, up and down. It may boil down to how well you control the quality of the product. With no sales increase, there is no extra money for the business. With no extra money for the business, there will be no extra money (bonus) for you. The better the product is to the customer, the more times they will come back to buy, which in turn, will increase your sales. As you can see, what this is getting to is that quality control is the focal part of your sales. Train your people to have the awareness as you have. You cannot be everywhere at once, which is why you hired your employees to be your second set of eyes. If they are trained properly, then you should have no problem in this area.

ATMOSPHERE

Atmosphere is a mindset of what you see, hear, and feel. Create an atmosphere that everyone would love to be a part of. You will be head of operations, and the business you run will be a reflection of you. The people you hire and how well you train them will be a reflection of you. Establish order and open communication among everyone first. Your employees will mainly be the faces your customers are interacting with. Your customers can sense when there is a good vibe going on in your store. How, you say? Your employees will show it in their work. It will show in how the product is received. It will show in how the employees relate with the customers as well as with their fellow co-workers. If it comes down to you having to play light, jazzy tunes to set the atmosphere, then do it. Whatever it takes to create the mood, then try it, to see if it would work. The cleanliness of your store tells about the pride your people put in it. Employees, as well as yourself, should be well-groomed and professional at all times. Encouraging them to respond with *"Yes, sir"* and *"No, ma'am"* will take your service to the next level of respect between you, the employees, and the customers. Respect your money. (Remember what I said money was earlier?)

SETTING STANDARDS

You are the coach of your team. You win games when you execute specific plays, night in and night out, to achieve your goal. Your motto is high-pressure defense, and that is what you stick by. You have proven fact, and your record that shows your method works, so no one should stray from it. The moment someone does, they will have the same effect on their teammate, which may cause a domino effect. In turn, that will be a game lost under your belt. Whether it is time standards, signing off on any checklist forms, following customer service procedures, or standards from your operations manual, everyone needs to know, *"This is how it is, and how it is going to be."* No questions asked.

Keep your mind open for suggestions that can help the business progress. Anything outside of that can be thrown out of the window. Your standards should never be personal; they should be for the better of the business. If someone asks you why, explain it to him or her versus simply telling them, *"Because I said so."* You are not being fair to them or your business by doing it that way. Explain to them the **whys** of why things are done a certain way. Once you have explained it to them properly, nine times out of ten, they will do it right. You need to look at standards like the freezing point. You cannot freeze any item above thirty-three degrees Fahrenheit; it's just not possible. You cannot deviate from the plan; your standards need to be *that* concrete. The moment you pull back on standards, like I said earlier, it can start a domino effect. Set the standards between manager and employee. They have to know that you are boss and that the buck stops here. Customers understand your standards after their first encounter. Whether it will be a good encounter or bad one will be determined by you. Everything you do will get to the customer, and then back to you, one way or the other. "Do it right the first time" will save you time.

Chapter Three

Hiring Staff

One of the most difficult parts of management is people management. Managing people can take its emotional toll on you. There are ups and downs, good times, bad times, relief, belief, or failure. You must keep the upper hand on all of these situations. Lots of businesses fail due to mismanaged employees. These people are the backbone of your business. Every manager wishes they can clone themselves; then everything would be a lot easier. Until that is legalized, this is the hand you are dealt. Mismanaged employees come from management not spending quality time with them to guarantee they know how to run the business consistently, day in and day out.

I've always believed in employee empowerment. If you don't involve them with things going on in their work environment, then how do you expect them to perform? What's the purpose of doing anything if you have no care for it? Who would it hurt for an employee to know how the business is doing, such as sales or total units? This information is valuable to you and the business as well as to the employee. This gives the employee a form a power, ownership, and responsibility they need. This will only help you out in the long run. You never know; simply getting them more involved may reveal your next lead employee, supervisor, or assistant manager. Now, that's power! Employees who know more last longer. Listen to your employees. Listen to their wants, needs, complaints, and concerns. If your workers aren't happy, then everything will go downhill. Your employees are living reflections of you. If something is done in your business, right or wrong, you take credit for it along with them.

Being the manager that I was, I hated to be misrepresented. I decided to get involved with my employees and train them the way I wanted them to be trained. Train them right from the get-go, as soon as you hire them. Take them through proper orientation and training classes when available. Don't expect everyone to know how to swim when you throw them in water. They may drown. Teach them how to swim, and teach them all different styles so they can be successful with everyone else. I know how it is, from firsthand experience, to be thrown into a situation when I don't know how to do anything. Even though I am a quick learner, the point is, I didn't know anything about the operation. How was I supposed to survive? Imagine an employee going through the same thing. They may not learn as quickly as others. Everyone has different learning curves. For example, I found out my senior year in high school, I had to do everything back-to-front to comprehend properly. I read the summary at the end of every chapter, then went back, page-by-page, to understand it. These are the things you have to be prepared for and have enough patience to deal with. You also have to have enough common sense to know when someone is pulling your leg and acting like they have lack of intelligence.

WHO TO LOOK FOR

What's the first step in finding a star employee? Only you know how many employees you need. They may be male, female, or a high school or college student (even though it is illegal to discriminate based on sex, age, gender, etc.) Once you figure that out, you can scratch that off step one.

THINGS TO BE AWARE OF WHEN LOOKING OVER APPLICATIONS

One of my rules is that if I can't pronounce your name, then your application will get looked over. I don't want to have to spend more than one minute trying to pronounce or enunciate your name.

HANDWRITING

If they can't take the time and care to fill out an application legibly, then how much time and care do you think they're going to apply at the job?

HOURS OF AVAILABILITY

Pay close attention when they write down the days they can't work. Are the days they can't work your busy days? How will these days work out for you? Did they write it down thinking for sure they were going to get the job? Even when I filled out applications, I would leave my availability open and discuss it during the interview.

EDUCATION

You wouldn't want someone who hasn't finished high school or received his or her G.E.D. handling your cash or accounting. (Some people are a little more gifted than others so there are exceptions.) Check if they are still enrolled in high school or college, or if they have graduated.

PAST WORK HISTORY

This will tell you their work habits, experience (vital if past work involves similarity to the position that needs to be filled). Check hourly wages, and if you can match that, or if what you pay is more or less than they are accustomed to.

DATES WORKED

Is this an employee who likes to job-hop every couple of months? Do they have a sob story behind every job they left? If so, there is your future drama queen or king. Longevity is also a good sign. If they have been with a company for over two years and decided to leave, maybe they're looking for a change of scenery.

REASON FOR LEAVING JOB

A typical answer for this one can be *"Not enough hours."* The question that pops in your head should be, "How many hours are they looking for and how many can I offer?" *"Didn't get along with management."* Do they have respect for authority? Did the manager or management team do something wrong? Not all of the time when they fill this out, the employee is in the wrong. Managers are human, too; we do make mistakes. *"School."* Couldn't they maintain a job and school? These are some of the things to look out for. Sometimes you may find an application where they have no work history at all. You could have the honor of being their first job.

THE INTERVIEW

By this time, you've seen your fair share of applications. Now it's time to make the decision on who to interview. Pick out three to five applicants whom you would like to interview. Write all of your notes on Post-its and stick them on the application. (Legally, you can't write on applications.) Things that should be written initially are the date, time called, and if you left a message (write down the name of the person who took the message if someone is to deliver it). If I were to call more than two times and my message didn't get returned, I would give up. Obviously, they didn't want the job. When I did get a hold of them, I would conduct a mini-interview over the phone. I would introduce myself and explain why I was calling. I would ask if they were still interested in the job. If so, I would ask a few brief questions, things like hours of availability, school, and where they are currently employed. I would do that to get an idea of who they were, right off the top. When it was time to set the interview, I would try to have it before the business opened (if their schedule allowed it).

Unless there is a valid reason, there shouldn't be any reason why they are late. That is the worst way to start an interview. Take notes on how early they show. As many people as I have interviewed, I have found that many show up early, usually twenty minutes. This is all to impress you. The question is,

"Is this who they really are?" You may not find out later down the road if this is the right one. People can be tricky. I've been burned, also. I thought I had a diamond but had coal. In an interview, I believe the person should talk more than you and keep steady eye contact. This rarely happens because the majority of applicants are so nervous answering questions to please you.

BODY LANGUAGE

Make them feel comfortable enough to open up to you when they are there. This starts with introducing yourself along with a formal handshake and smile. If you don't know the handshake rule, here it is. An extra firm handshake shows they're very aggressive. A soft handshake shows they're very laid back. Try to look for one between the two. You will know within the first five minutes if this is the person for you. Here are some typical questions to start off with. Eventually, you will come up with your own questions that will appeal to you and business.

"TELL ME ABOUT YOURSELF"

See which angle they take on this one. Some will take the business approach, some will take the personal, and some will ask you to clarify. The third option can be taken two ways. Do they have a brain? Do they want you to be specific on what you're asking? What do you think? You know the answer to these questions. You're the one conducting the interview. I can't tell you what you're looking for. You're on your own on this one.

"WHAT KIND OF HOURS ARE YOU LOOKNG FOR?"

Day shift? Night shift? Open availability? Fifteen or thirty hours a week? What hours can you offer them?

This is just as critical as showing up on time. You have to see what their views of management are. As they tell you about past management, you will learn about how other businesses run and treat employees. There will be mixed reviews. I always took this as a self-evaluation. I would ask myself, "Do we do that here? Have I ever done that?" Encourage them to go into detail about their work experience, experience with management, and various hierarchy systems they have experienced. Ask them how they dealt with co-workers and customers.

*"OUT OF ALL THE APPLICATIONS
THAT I HAVE, WHY SHOULD I PICK
YOU? WHAT CAN YOU BRING
TO THE TEAM THAT WE DON'T*

ALREADY HAVE?"

Most will try to be humble and answer this how they think you would want it answered. This is a question of confidence. If they really want the job, you would see it in this answer.

THE DECISION

Which one do you go for? Words of advice? I have none. You have one interviewee who has a great personality but no work experience. On the other hand, you have "vice versa" applicant. It all depends on what you're looking for. I've come to learn that the ones with work experience tend to last longer. At the same time, when they understand the ins and outs about the business (which is usually about two to three months), they may quit. I never could understand why this would happen. The ones with little or no work experience may take longer to train.

They require more supervision, but on the plus side, you can mold them into what you want, and best of all, they're not ruined by past jobs or employers. You have the honor in starting their work career off right. As stated earlier, "Your employees are a reflection of you." Mold them correctly, manage them well, and give them as much attention as they need in order for your business to run efficiently. You can give staff all the attention in the world, or be so nice to them it hurts. It never fails; one out of three new hires will quit in a two- to three-month period. The good ones, I mean the really good ones, will actually give you notice. The majority of the time, it will come up in a no call/no show for shifts. Calling them will do no good because they have already made up their mind. You may question yourself, "Is it something I did?" You did nothing wrong (unless you're a horrible boss). Do not get depressed about it. You have to take your lumps. This is where the interviewees that you didn't hire will come in handy. Always keep one in your back pocket for situations like these. Circumstances like these will come up when you least expected. You can't let this get the better of you. What doesn't kill you will make you stronger.

Chapter Four

Store Cleanliness

The cleanliness of your business reflects your personality. It will reflect the amount of care you have for the place. It may sound strange, but it's true: if you are not organized enough to notice the cleanliness of the store, you lack awareness. Unless you have procedures already in place to clean items, and what to use, you will need to create them. Let's call it your *cleaning list (daily, weekly, monthly)*. "How do you come up with procedures?" you ask. Once again, it is up to you. You need to dedicate time to go through your establishment to see what needs to be cleaned, how, with what, and how often. The first step in this process is to gather your almighty planner (we will talk about this in Chapter 5) so you can write all of this down. Start at the very back of your store and slowly make your way up to the front. This all has to be done **"YOUR"** way. Everything needs to be checked, from the doors to the thresholds, employee break rooms, restrooms, counter area, and reception table.

Let's start with your restrooms. Everyone (at least I do) hates a dirty bathroom. How clean is it overall? If a customer needed to use it, would they feel comfortable in it? It is called *rest*room. OK, what do I clean it with? A multi-surface cleaning agent, or some form of chlorine bleach? *Use something that will clean, obviously, and that smells clean (but not to a point where if someone was to come in they would faint* *from the fumes).* How would you clean it? Spray, wipe, or scrub? How much toilet paper should you have and do you have enough of it? If you were to run out, do you have a backup in there? Sinks, mirrors, and garbage cans need to be examined routinely. I think you get the gist of it now.

You have to answer these questions and come up with plan for each individual area of your establishment that will ensure these items are attended to, properly, with the right cleansers, and in routine. Do not hold back when writing this down. Go into as much detail as needed. If you do not set the standard, then it will never get done the correct way.

Once you are done finding all of the areas and how they are to be cleaned, you are ready to form your cleaning list. Have a sign-off sheet next to each item for the staff to check off when they have completed an item from the list. Post this sheet in an open area, or in a binder, so no one will have an excuse on why they couldn't find the list. When the health department comes for their inspection, you shouldn't have any worries. By now, you have your procedures in place that you have no worries and will pass with flying colors. Keep your health department scores on file so you can have a record on when they came, what they saw, and what improvements are needed.

You are the overseer, not the actual laborer (well, you *shouldn't* be, but things happen). Make you job easier by assigning someone or two to be in charge of the cleaning list. Once they've taken the list, and delegated it out amongst the rest of the staff, your job is to come in to see if it was done to your standards. This is only done after you have walked someone else (someone within your management team) through your inspection that you have done to create this form. They need to be on accord and share your vision. Everyone needs to see what you see. Cleanliness of your business is the first thing customers notice when they come to you. Put yourself in the shoes of the customer. If you're are not comfortable with it, then nine times out of ten, they won't be either. You may have to get a janitor to do your cleaning, or hire a cleaning service to come in at night, but for the most part, the staff does the upkeep work. Pull out that cleaning list when there is stand around time. As long as there is air to breathe, there will be something to clean.

Chapter Five

DAILY PLANNER/ORGANIZER

THE KEY FEATURE OF AN ELITE MANAGER IS HOW ORGANIZED YOU KEEP YOURSELF. You will have different ideas going through your head at all times. You may see tasks that need to be completed, cleaning duties, or innovative ideas that will help you and your business run that much better. First off, you will need to purchase a daily planner/organizer. They can run from $30 to more than $150. (I personally have a Franklin Covey, if you want to know.) The work it will do for you will be priceless, so consider it a lifelong investment. This can be used to jot down ideas and goals or a to-do list, to remind yourself of appointments set, writing down goals, to do list, or serve as your own personal journal. It will help you out in more ways than you can imagine. Once you've purchased your planner, you will need to familiarize yourself with it. Customize it to fit your needs. Put something of value in it such as your identification, checkbook or credit cards, so you will not forget it. Otherwise, if you do not put any value in it, you will never use it. Just think of it as an extension to your wallet or purse, but with more capabilities. You never know where you're going to be when an idea hits you, or when you will need to write down a contact's name.

Now that you have familiarized and customized your planner, it is up to you to use it. Discipline yourself to use the planner. Set aside five to ten minutes before you start your day to jot down how you want your day to go. At the end of your day, double-check your planner to see if your day went how you wrote it out to be. If you did not complete all of your goals or tasks, it is OK; just transfer the items that you did not complete to the next day. The items transferred from the previous day are prioritized first on the list to guarantee their completion.

WEEKLY NOTES

Weekly notes were my version of a newsletter with all store information for my employees to read. It can contain whatever information you want it to have. It can range from weekly sales reviews, new procedures, operations, customer complaints, and follow-up. This is therapeutic, in its own way. You can relieve stress through writing these items down. At times, you may need to vent or talk to everyone at once, and this is the perfect medium to achieve this. As your day progresses, keep your planner open, or if possible, on you at all times. If you have any information valuable from procedure changes or any topics that I named above, then write it down. It can be something simple as, *"Be sure to clock in and out properly on time cards."* You may have this problem with one or more employees, and this is the way you can address this all in one shot. It doesn't have to be all business, all the time. You can write down fun stuff also, such as employee anniversaries, birthdays, or employee-of-the-month recognition. All of your employees may not know it's Steven's two-year anniversary this week, or that the store has seen the best sales in six months. This is all valuable information that needs to be spread to everyone. At the end of your note, there needs to be an area for employees to sign off at when they are done reading. That way you will know who has and has not read them.

By the end of the week, your planner should have scribbles and ideas jotted down. Set aside a day where you can go back to put all of this information in order and make sense of it to create your notes. I would recommend typing them if you have time. Your handwriting may not be that legible for everyone to understand. Some things you may not be able to remember what you were even talking about because you wrote it down so quickly. This tends to happen, but take a few moments to reflect on what point you were trying to get across and then you will be able to remember.

Once you've completed your notes, then hang them up in a designated place, preferably in the break area. Keeping employees involved in business activity and even with you is an excellent formula for low turnover and longevity. For some employees, they may not want to be that involved and that is OK, but do not let that one get away from you or spoil it for everyone else. The notes are a way for all to keep up with the business and the progress it is making. If that employee cannot keep up through the notes, and it affects their performance with their job, then their job is in jeopardy.

Your notes need to be taken seriously. Set the bar with them and let everyone know the severity of information with them. You should issue out your notes at least once a week or every two. It depends on you and how much you want your employees to know. Words from the wise: "The more they know, the more you all will grow."

OFFICE TIME

It is important to spend quality time in the office. You have to do it within the demands of the business. Some days you may have more time than others. When the opportunity comes, take it, and use it wisely. The operation relies on you to know when it is doing well, and when it is not. There has to be a time when you have to gather yourself to grasp the business. When I say **grasp the business**, it means knowing what is going on. You cannot run an efficient operation with no knowledge of your surroundings. Do you have enough staff for the season? Do you have a cash/short problem? If so, are there procedures in place to catch a thief? Do you have enough office supplies? Is your inventory coming up short? Is your operational cost meeting or exceeding the budget? These are the questions you need to know, have an answer or a solution to, or at least, one in the works.

The office is your den within your home. You want it to be organized and in place, so when you need anything from there, you and everyone else know exactly where it is. All of your files need to be kept in folders in the filing cabinet, labeled and dated. Arrange files within the folder in an orderly fashion. Post a guide on the filing cabinet to display which order the files go in. Keep copies of sale reports from current and prior years. Prior-year files will help you predict current business trends, which in turn, assist you for your operation to run smoothly. Supplies such as copies of cleaning lists, job aids, postage stamps, or ink pens & pencils should be kept with par levels like you do inventory. Having par levels for your office supplies helps you so when it comes to purchase supplies, you know what to build to.

Office time is based on what you do with it when you get it. Personally, I spent so much time dealing with the public and physically running the operation, that I barely had enough time as I would like in the office. And honestly, that will be you. I cannot pinpoint exactly what you need to do. It is about how you customize it to fit your schedules. Sorry, you are on your own for this one. This is when the planner comes in, because you should have been writing down your to do list for when you got office time.

Closure

I am glad to see that you have completed the book. I tried my best not to make it long. I know you have other things you could have been doing, but you took time out to better yourself, and I respect that. This is the first step to becoming better at what you do. And you know what? That effort alone shows that you are more than ready for your future as a manager. I hope that I have done you some service. I felt that it was in your best interest that I shared my experience with you. I wanted to put you in a mindset of what to prepare for.

Some of the angles I came at stemmed from negative results. Take it as pruning. You got to cut some of the bad stuff for it to grow right. Coming from a guy who came from the bottom of the ranks to the top, I know what it takes to get there. I am still learning, just as you are. Remember this: You are great, and you will do great things. If something doesn't go the right way, keep on ticking. Life goes on and everything you do is a learning experience. Utilize what is around you to take ownership in your work. I exploited my practice to write this book. I knew someone out there would have some of the initial questions that I had. This book is for you, and people like you. This is the first stage of many you are going to go through at your position. Keep striving for perfection and finding ways for improvement. CREATE REALITY – IT'S A VERB! You dictate what goes on from here.

Notes and Quotes

As a manager, there will always be ideas floating in your head. This is why I stated earlier the need for a daily planner. As I neared completion of this book, I began to think about things to add here and there, ideas that I would like to share with you.

-NEVER LET LABOR BUDGETS GET IN THE WAY OF CUSTOMER SERVICE.

-NEVER LET ADMINISTRATIVE/OFFICE WORK GET IN THE WAY OF CUSTOMER SERVICE.

-WHEN IT COMES TO PRODUCT, IT IS BETTER TO HAVE IT AND NOT NEED IT, THAN NEED IT AND NOT HAVE IT.

-THE MORE PEOPLE YOU HAVE ON STAFF, THE MORE PERSONALITIES YOU WILL HAVE TO JUGGLE.

-TRAIN AS MANY PEOPLE AS YOU SEE FIT TO DO YOUR JOB. IT WILL ONLY HELP YOU OUT IN THE LONG RUN.

-IF YOU SEE A PROBLEM, FIX IT THEN AND THERE. NEVER LET IT CARRY OVER TO THE NEXT DAY.

-DO NOT LET SITUATIONS FESTER INSIDE OF YOU. WRITE THEM DOWN OR ADDRESS THEM.

-WORK SMARTER, NOT HARDER.

-THE TIME YOU INVEST INTO YOUR OPERATION IS WHAT YOU WILL RECEIVE BACK.

-"YES, SIR" AND "YES, MA'AM" EXTENDS THE LINE OF RESPECT WITH CUSTOMERS AND EMPLOYEES.

-T.E.A.M. (TOGETHER EMPLOYEES AND MANAGEMENT) = SUCCESS.

-EVERY DAY, IT'S SOMETHING. AS DIFFERENT AS THE DAYS OF THE WEEK ARE, SO WILL YOUR SITUATIONS BE.

-ENSURE THAT THERE IS A TRAINING CHECKLIST TO VERIFY THAT ALL EMPLOYEES ARE PROPERLY TRAINED. WHEN TRAINING IS COMPLETE, THE CHECKLIST SHOULD BE COMPLETED ALSO.

-THE GOOD AND BAD FALL ON YOU.

-TAKE ADVANTAGE OF EVERY OPPORTUNITY TO PROMOTE YOUR OPERATION. IN THE END, IT WILL BE MORE MONEY IN YOUR POCKET.

-PREPARE TO WORK LONG HOURS, BE ON CALL, AND COVER SOMEONE'S SHIFT.

-YOUR DIET MAY CHANGE. TRY NOT TO LET IT GET OUT OF CONTROL.

-HAVE SOMETHING TO SHOW FOR ALL THE WORK YOU HAVE PUT IN. NEVER WORK IN VAIN.

-"ASK" YOUR EMPLOYEES. TRY NOT TO DEMAND.

-YOU ARE THE LEADER, OTHERS WILL FOLLOW.

CREATEREALITY
IT'S A VERB!   TM

FOR FURTHER INFORMATION ON PURCHASING A T-SHIRT OR RINGER SHIRT WITH THIS LOGO PLEASE CONTACT

CHRISTIAN EVANS
CREATE REALITY, INC
PO BOX 9665
PEORIA, IL 61612-9665

FEEL FREE TO EMAIL
createreality_inc@yahoo.com

T-SHIRTS- $18

RINGER SHIRTS- $21

Additional Information

If you would like Christian Evans to speak to you, or your organization, please contact:

Christian Evans
CREATE REALITY, INC.
P.O. BOX 9665
PEORIA, IL 61612-9965

Phone: **309-648-5355**
Email: **createreality_inc@yahoo.com**
Web: **www.createreality-inc.com**

For additional copies of A MANAGERS MIND please make a $10 check or money order payable to CREATE REALITY, INC. and send it to the address listed above. Allow two to four weeks for delivery. We'll pay for the shipping☺

ABOUT THE AUTHOR

Founding his company CREATE REALITY, INC., Christian J. Evans is an entrepreneur. Serving as President & CEO, this book is the first of many great creations to come. At 24 years wiser, he has started a company with a movement -Using your imagination to create and pushing yourself to see your dreams come true. "I've always written since I was young. Jotting stuff down here and there, or constantly writing out thoughts on how I felt about a particular situation. Now I have a chance to share that with you. I've used my imagination to create for the world to see. If you have something you want to get out, then do it. CREATE REALITY- IT'S A VERB!"

www.ingramcontent.com/pod-product-compliance
Lightning Source LLC
Chambersburg PA
CBHW022119170526
45157CB00004B/1692

*9 7 8 1 4 2 5 9 0 2 0 6 3 *